Nos encantan las ciencias
So Into Science!

EXPLOREMOS EL BOSQUE

EXPLORING THE FOREST

Marie Roesser
Traducido por / Translated by Eida de la Vega

Gareth Stevens Publishing

Please visit our website, www.garethstevens.com. For a free color catalog of all our high-quality books, call toll free 1-800-542-2595 or fax 1-877-542-2596.

Library of Congress Cataloging-in-Publication Data

Names: Roesser, Marie, author.
Title: Exploring the forest = Exploremos el bosque / Marie Roesser.
Description: New York : Gareth Stevens Publishing, [2019] | Series: So into science! = Nos encantan las ciencias | Includes index.
Identifiers: LCCN 2018013143| ISBN 9781538236369 (library bound)
Subjects: LCSH: Forest ecology–Juvenile literature. | Forest animals–Juvenile literature. | Forest plants–Juvenile literature.
Classification: LCC QH541.5.F6 R64 2019 | DDC 577.3–dc23
LC record available at https://lccn.loc.gov/2018013143

Published in 2019 by
Gareth Stevens Publishing
111 East 14th Street, Suite 349
New York, NY 10003

Translator: Eida de la Vega
Editor, English: Therese Shea
Designer: Sarah Liddell

Photo credits: Cover, p. 1 Piotr Krzeslak/Shutterstock.com; p. 5 Olga Danylenko/Shutterstock.com; p. 7 (maple tree) Dave Allen Photography/Shutterstock.com; p. 7 (maple seed) SAJE/Shutterstock.com; p. 9 (oak tree) Aleksey Stemmer/Shutterstock.com; pp. 9, 24 (acorns) Dionisvera/Shutterstock.com; p. 11 (pine trees) Jeff Zehnder/Shutterstock.com; p. 11 (pine needles) xpixel/Shutterstock.com; p. 13 rsooll/Shutterstock.com; p. 15 LesPalenik/Shutterstock.com; p. 17 Peter Krejzl/Shutterstock.com; p. 19 Andrey Pavlov/Shutterstock.com; p. 21 Dirk Ercken/Shutterstock.com; p. 23 Monkey Business Images/Shutterstock.com; p. 24 (rain forest) AustralianCamera/Shutterstock.com.

Printed in the United States of America

CPSIA compliance information: Batch #CW19GS: For further information contact Gareth Stevens, New York, New York at 1-800-542-2595.

Contenido

Contents

Estamos en un bosque.
Un bosque tiene
muchos árboles.

We are in a forest!
A forest has many trees.

Este es un arce.
Sus semillas
se llaman sámaras.

••••••••••••••••••••••••••••••

This is a maple.
Its seeds are called keys!

Este es un roble.
Sus semillas
se llaman bellotas.

• •

This is an oak.
Its seeds are acorns!

Los pinos siempre
están verdes.
No tienen hojas.
Tienen agujas.

....

Pines are always green.
They don't have leaves.
They have needles.

Hay más plantas
en el bosque.
¡Veo flores silvestres!

There are more
forest plants.
I see wildflowers!

Los osos pardos
viven en los bosques.
Los osos grizzly
son osos pardos.

....

Brown bears live
in forests.
Grizzly bears are
brown bears!

Los búhos viven
en los bosques.
El gran búho gris
es el más grande.

• •

Owls live in forests.
The great gray owl
is the biggest owl!

Los insectos ayudan
a que los bosques crezcan.
Las hormigas
llevan semillas.

Bugs help forests grow.
Ants carry seeds.

Las ranas viven
en los bosques.
Las ranas de los
bosques tropicales
son de muchos colores.

Frogs live in forests.
Frogs in rain forests
are many colors!

¡Me encanta el bosque!

• •

I love the forest!

Palabras que debes aprender
Words to Know

(la) bellota
acorn

(el) bosque tropical
rain forest

Índice / Index